COLOMBIA'S TREATMENT
OF FOREIGN BANKS

COLOMBIA'S TREATMENT OF FOREIGN BANKS

A Precedent Setting Case?

James E. Boyce
François J. Lombard

90116

American Enterprise Institute for Public Policy Research
Washington, D. C.

James E. Boyce is professor of management at Michigan Technological University. François J. Lombard is assistant professor of business administration at the Université de Droit, d'Economie, et des Sciences d'Aix-Marseille.

ISBN 0-8447-3212-5

Foreign Affairs Study 36, May 1976

Library of Congress Catalog Card No. 76-12153

Printed in the United States of America

CONTENTS

INTRODUCTION

Somewhere near the top of anyone's list of the world's serious problems must be the growing gap between the richer and the poorer nations. One part of that problem—and a focus of considerable nationalistic sentiment—is the relationship between the governments of the poorer countries and the multinational corporations domiciled in (and controlled from) the richer. Among the important multinational corporations operating in the Third World countries (which include almost all the poorer countries in which multinational corporations would find it worthwhile to operate) are the multinational banks.

The Focus of this Study. Not all the Third World countries have substantial democratic traditions. Consequently, when the democratically elected government of a respected Third World country takes a step toward radically changing the status of the multinational banks operating within its boundaries, that step may be considered important, not only for the country and the banks, but indeed for the development of multinational business and the Third World generally. Such a step was taken by the government of Colombia with the promulgation of Decree 295 in February 1975.

The nub of Decree 295 is that multinational banks operating in Colombia should agree to convert their Colombian branches to a "mixed" status—which is to say that they should sell 51 percent of their stock to Colombian nationals. The bank managers who have been asked to convert are quite naturally wondering where this first step will lead. Moreover, the question of conversion is related to larger questions: How will the Colombian case affect other countries in Latin America? What is the best policy for multinational banks

1

to follow in the future? And, from the Colombian standpoint, how can Colombia have acceptable control over its own future and still attract (or indeed retain) foreign investment capital sufficient for economic development?

The study that follows was designed to explore the relationship between the government and the multinational banks in Colombia in the light of Decree 295, with the larger questions kept in mind. It should also contribute to communication between the government and the banks, thereby helping to provide a realistic decision-making basis for the parties involved. Once the historical parameters of the problem were established, the method of research employed was the conducting of "off-the-record" interviews with representatives of multinational banks operating in Colombia (which we will hereafter speak of as "foreign banks"), representatives of domestic Colombian banks, and representatives of the Colombian government. Evidently, the representatives of the domestic banks might be expected to hold a middle position between the foreign banks and the government.

The study begins with a brief review of the history of foreign investment in Colombia in general (Section 1) and of foreign banking in Colombia in particular (Section 2). Section 3 presents the results of the survey, the differing perceptions and views involved. In Section 4 we attempt to look ahead, putting the current issues in the broader perspective, while making a few specific recommendations. Before we turn to the history of foreign investment, however, it may be worthwhile, in this introduction, to take a brief look at the past history of Colombian–U.S. relationships.

Past Relations between the United States and Colombia. The Republic of Colombia was first among the liberated colonies of Spain to be recognized as independent, and the United States was the first government outside Latin America to recognize that independent status.[1] Later, in 1848, the United States approved a treaty guaranteeing Colombian sovereignty over the isthmus of Panama. At the turn of the century, the United States negotiated a treaty with Colombia to build a canal through the isthmus.

> But when the treaty was rejected by the Colombian Senate, the U.S. supported a revolution for the independence of Panama, which broke out in 1903. The revolutionary government promptly signed a treaty with the U.S., which not only granted Washington sweeping rights to build and

---

[1] Dexter Perkins, *The United States and Latin America* (Baton Rouge: Louisiana State University Press, 1961), p. 47.

defend a canal, but which for all practical purposes made Panama a U.S. protectorate.[2]

These American activities during and immediately following the Panama revolution caused long-lasting bitter feelings toward the United States among Colombians. From the time of these headline events until well into the 1920s, American public opinion was divided on whether the government had acted properly towards Colombia, a division evidenced by the opposing views expressed during heated debates in the U.S. Senate. However, in 1921, the U.S. Senate finally ratified the Urrutia–Thompson treaty, which included an indemnity payment of $25 million to Colombia for the loss of Panama. One of the reasons for opposition to this treaty was the contention that the payment was an indirect subsidy to U.S. oil interests.[3]

During the 1920s many Latin American countries wanted the United States to accept the doctrine that no nation has the right to intervene in the domestic or foreign affairs of any other nation. For some years, the U.S. government resisted, but changed its stand and officially accepted this "Good Neighbor" policy in 1933.[4] Nevertheless, despite the "Good Neighbor" policy, two fundamental changes produced increased tension in relations between the United States and Latin America after World War II. The first was a shift in U.S. policy whereby Latin America was relegated from a primary to a secondary role, as a result of U.S. "worldwide engagement." The second was the fact that Latin American leaders were beginning programs of rapid economic development and looking to the United States for assistance at the very time the United States was preoccupied elsewhere. During the 1950s U.S.–Latin American relations deteriorated seriously.[5]

Furthermore, though this was a manifestation of a long-standing difference, Latin Americans disagreed with the approach of the U.S. government toward economic development strategy. Washington advocated a "free enterprise" system, while many Latin American officials favored more government-directed and planned economic systems. Centralized governmental control with complex bureaucratic structures had in fact been established in Latin America from the earliest decades of colonial government, and U.S. leaders even in the period of the Latin American revolutions had noted the funda-

---

[2] Arthur M. Schlesinger, Jr., ed., *The Dynamics of World Power: A Documentary History of United States Foreign Policy, 1945-1973* (New York: Chelsea House, 1973), vol. 3 (Robert N. Burr, *Latin America*), p. xxii.

[3] E. Taylor Parks, *Colombia and the United States* (Durham, N.C.: Duke University Press, 1935), pp. ix, 395, 429, 451, 457.

[4] Perkins, *The United States and Latin America*, p. 24.

[5] Burr, *Latin America*, pp. xix, xxxii.

mental differences between North American and Latin American traditions—not always, to be sure, in terms complimentary to the latter.[6]

In 1961, under President Kennedy's aegis, the Organization of American States established the Alliance for Progress, attempting thereby to coordinate and direct toward common goals the divergent (and perhaps irreconcilable) U.S. and Latin American views on economic development.[7] The Alliance for Progress may have helped create the atmosphere in which there took place extensive cultural exchanges between the United States and the countries of Latin America, including Colombia. One may note the irony implicit in the fact that Colombia took the lead among Latin American countries in accepting U.S. Peace Corps volunteers in that pleasant atmosphere of the 1960s and now, in the 1970s, is taking the lead among countries in Latin America in requiring "mixed" status for U.S. (and other) multinational banks.[8]

1. FOREIGN INVESTMENT IN COLOMBIA

In some ways, Colombia is a typical less-developed country, although, unlike many less-developed countries, it has a liberal and democratic tradition. Among the Andean countries, Colombia is considered a leader and its capital, Bogotá, has at times been referred to as the Athens of Latin America.[9] These two points—that Colombia is in many ways a typical less-developed country, and that Columbia is a leader among Andean nations—should be kept in mind in the discussion that follows.

The History of Foreign Investment in Colombia. The treatment of foreign investment in Colombia has been determined by the interaction of at least four factors:[10] the historical role played by foreign

---

6 Claudia Veliz, ed., *Latin America and the Caribbean: A Handbook* (New York: Frederick A. Praeger, 1968), p. xx. On the differences between North America and Latin America, see for example the comments of John Adams in C. F. Adams, ed., *The Works of John Adams*, vol. 10 (Boston: Little, Brown & Co., 1856), pp. 144-145.

7 Burr, *Latin America*, p. xliii.

8 Thomas E. Weil, et al., *Area Handbook of Colombia* (Washington, D.C.: U.S. Government Printing Office, 1970), pp. 298, 304, on the Peace Corps in Colombia.

9 "Investing, Trading and Licensing in Colombia," *Business International* (May 1973).

10 See François Lombard, "Toward a Methodology to Select Foreign Direct Investment—The Host Country Point of View—Case of Colombia" (Ph.D. diss., Wharton School of Finance, in progress).

census was that there was a need to establish better control over foreign investment and a need to require foreign investors to sell their foreign currency to the Central Bank, register their capital with the Foreign Exchange Board, inform the Chamber of Commerce of their operations, and invest in an economic sector beneficial to the country generally.[22]

Within this framework, the corporations were not prohibited from carrying out intercompany transactions, nor were they prohibited from declaring as capital imports all sorts of intangibles and good will. But a study made in 1950 by the Ministry of Finance showed that, of 1,031 foreign firms in Colombia, about 50 percent, 533 exactly, did not have adequate financial statements or keep adequate books.

The industrialization of Colombia and growth of foreign investment, 1950–1975. During the period from 1950 to 1975, foreign investment and especially U.S. investment in Colombia grew substantially. There were at least three factors that help explain the development of foreign ventures: tariff restrictions, technological considerations, and issues of competition.

At the beginning of the 1950s, Colombia, advised by the UN Economic Commission for Latin America (ECLA) and especially by Raúl Prebisch, began a policy of import-substitution. The purpose of this policy was to develop an industrial base in order to avoid importing increasingly expensive manufactured goods, and eventually to build local industries able to compete in the world markets, thereby diversifying exports.

The first step was to protect the infant industries and establish tariff barriers. For the international firms, this new policy had two effects: importing goods into Colombia became more expensive, and a monopoly position was given to the first firms to be established. This explains, for example, why most of the foreign pharmaceutical companies established plants in Colombia after 1951. Of 170 pharmaceutical companies in Colombia, the 32 foreign firms produce 75 percent of all the goods produced. In the chemical sector, the major foreign firm, Celanese, came in 1950, and 70 percent of the existing foreign firms made their first investments between 1958 and 1966. In the paper industry, three out of four firms came between 1957 and 1964. In the food industry, Nestlé came to Colombia in 1945 and Corn Products in 1961 by acquiring a local firm, Fruco.

---

[22] Resolution 175 of 1947 completed by Decree 1949 of 1948.

During this period, Colombia tried to control the inflow of foreign exchange, especially for balance of payments purposes, and a series of decrees was passed to regulate the registration of past and present investment [23] and the right to repatriate capital.[24] These decrees lacked specific controls because of the absence of a specialized institution for control, and because the government did not realize the financial costs of any loophole in the institutional framework.[25]

One factor explaining the growth of foreign investment during this period is technology. An argument presented by Raymond Vernon [26] suggests that multinational corporations which have developed new products and new technology will build plants both in other developed countries and in less-developed countries in order to take advantage of cheaper labor costs, extended markets, and economies of scale. Another factor (not mentioned by Vernon) explaining the growth of foreign investment in Colombia would be the desire of the international firm to diversify earnings on a geographical basis and to maximize the growth of sales. The growth of the foreign financial sectors in Colombia can be seen in this perspective and will be described in the next section. These factors would explain the growth of foreign investments in electrical equipment manufacture in Colombia—for instance, the recent investments by Siemens S.A., International Business Machines, and Telemécanique. Total investment in the electrical equipment field amounted to $28 million (U.S.) in 1967 and in the years from 1967 to 1970 it amounted to $2.7 million (U.S.), a little less than foreign investment in the chemical and petroleum sector.[27]

Colombia's government became worried about foreign investment in 1967 when the country faced a serious balance of payments problem. The import-substitution policy required costly additional imports, especially imports of machinery. The government became

[23] Decrees 637 and 545 of 1951, Law 1a. of 1959.

[24] Decree 1625 of 1951, Law 8a. of 1952, Decree 107 of 1957, in Miguel Betancour, Dario Abad and Fred Castaño, "Inversión Extranjera en Colombia," pp. 60-61.

[25] Various studies have come to this conclusion, among them the study by Constantine Vaitsos that has shown the danger of transfer-pricing practices. The Colombian subsidiaries of the MNCs in such sectors as rubber, chemicals, electronics and pharmaceuticals overprice their intermediate products by 40, 25.5, 16 and 155 percent respectively. The local companies were thus selling at a much higher price than the international price. See Constantine V. Vaitsos, *Intercountry Income Distribution and Transnational Enterprises* (Oxford, England: Clarendon Press, 1974), p. 47.

[26] Raymond Vernon, "International Investment and International Trade in the Product Cycle," *Quarterly Journal of Economics*, vol. 74, no. 2 (May 1960), p. 80.

[27] Betancour, Abad, and Castaño, "Inversión Extranjera en Colombia," p. 66.

concerned about the balance of payments because the country faced some difficulties in dealing with the International Monetary Fund (IMF).[28] In fact, the foreign exchange constraint was identified as the key bottleneck slowing the country's economic growth.[29] The role of foreign investment was evaluated according to its impact on the balance of payments issue.

In the late 1960s Colombian officials and independent economists tried to evaluate the impact of foreign investment in Colombia. They came up with a diagnosis concerning which a lawyer who represented various international firms in Colombia made these comments:[30]

> Until March 22, 1967, the date in which Decree 444 of 1967 went into effect, there were practically no controls in Colombia over foreign investment as such.

> Under those conditions it became common in Colombia for a foreign corporation to establish a wholly-owned subsidiary or a branch, with a limited imported capital investment, and then proceed to finance its Colombian operations through local loans, which loans could even be guaranteed by the parent company. Colombian financial institutions were delighted to lend monies to these subsidiaries or branches of large international concerns, which in all cases constituted blue-chip clientele for the creditor.

> Another method for extracting additional profits from the country by foreign concerns, up to March of 1967, was through license agreements for the use of trademarks, patents and/or know-how and the rendering of technical services, which agreements would be executed by the parent company, as licensor, and the Colombian subsidiary or branch, as licensee.

> The above two systems have been highly criticized by local authorities and have been used as examples of how large international concerns come into a country not for the benefit of the country itself, but for their exclusive profit.

> Other common systems for extracting profits, such as marking up the price of raw materials of finished goods which

---

[28] See R. L. Maullin, *The Colombian IMF Disagreement of November–December 1966: An Interpretation of its Place in Colombian Politics* (Santa Monica: The Rand Corporation, 1967), and T. Hayter, *Aid as Imperialism* (Harmondsworth, Middlesex, and Baltimore, Maryland: Penguin, 1971), pp. 107-119.

[29] Jaroslev Vanek, *Estimating Foreign Exchange Needs* (New York: McGraw-Hill, 1968).

[30] James W. F. Raisbeck, "Foreign Investments: Do They Have a Future in Colombia?" *Colombian–American Business Review*, vol. 12, no. 53 (July-September 1972), p. 30.

the parent or one of its affiliated companies sends to the Colombian company, have not only been highly criticized, but have also been considered to be in violation of the exchange control regulations, and upon investigations which have taken place, mainly in the pharmaceutical industry to date, to have given rise to strong sanctions imposed on local subsidiaries of large international corporations.

Many of the critics do not seem to realize that what the international concerns were doing was absolutely legal: there were no prohibitions of any kind against a foreign corporation establishing a Colombian company with a small capital base and then proceeding to operate through local loans. Neither were there prohibitions against a foreign parent licensing, e.g., its trademarks, to its subsidiary for a certain royalty; nor likewise in respect to any markup in the price of goods sold.

Consequently, if allowing foreign enterprises to operate in the country under such highly favourable circumstances not subject to any controls was prejudicing Colombia, the question that must be asked is, who was at fault? Was it the foreign investors? I must very respectfully say that if anyone was at fault it was the past governments and/or legislatures which . . . allowed foreign investment to operate with no control whatsoever.

In 1967, Decree Law (Decreto Ley) 444 was passed, setting up a system for the regulation of foreign investment—a system that later served as a model in drafting Decision 24 of the Andean Pact. It may be noted that Colombia was influential in drafting Decision 24 of the Andean Pact, which established common treatment for foreign capital, trademarks, and patents within the Andean subregion. This influence came partly from the role played by the Colombian president (Dr. Carlos Lleras Restrepo) and his representatives in promoting the Andean Common Market, partly from Colombia's institutional experience in dealing with foreign investment, and partly from the research conducted in Colombia.

An Institutional Framework for Foreign Investment: Decree 444.

The control of foreign investment was one of the methods by which the government sought to improve the balance of payments. In 1966 President Lleras Restrepo appointed a commission to prepare measures to solve the foreign exchange problem. This commission suggested a policy of import controls and export promotion. Furthermore, in order "to promote economic and social development and exchange

12

equilibrium," Colombia, according to the decree, intended "to stimulate the investment of foreign capital in harmony with national economic interest."[31]

The contents of the decree and its implications. Decree Law 444 involved the interaction of at least four institutions. The National Planning Board (Departamento Nacional de Planeación) analyzes and approves investment proposals.[32] The Exchange Office (Oficina de Cambios) registers and authorizes the outflow of capital. The office also has the power to authorize contracts for technical assistance. The Superintendent of Foreign Commerce (El Director del Instituto de Comercio Exterior) grants import licenses.[33] The Advisory Committee on Global Licenses (Comité Asesor de Licencias Globales) is in charge of implementing the government policies on imports of capital goods and of avoiding an excess of unused productive capacity.[34] (A final step—added later—is registration of a foreign company with the superintendent of companies,[35] in order to inform the Colombian authorities about the status and social objectives of the company.)

The purpose of the Committee on Global Licenses is to see whether a proposal fits within the government's development plans. The committee works with the Foreign Investment Division of the National Planning Board and with the Royalty Committee, whose role is to analyze contracts involving the payment of royalties by Colombian firms obtaining technology from abroad. Its decisions are based on sixteen criteria, including specification of the product imported, the price, and the quality of information supplied. So far, the labor-intensity of the technology imported has not been considered.

---

[31] See Article 1, Decree-Law No. 444 of March 22, 1967.

[32] Within the context of Colombian politics, President Lleras Restrepo gave a key instrument to his economists in the Departamento Nacional de Planeación. The success of the foreign investment policy in Colombia has been due partly to the "honesty and the great technical ability" of civil servants of Planeación Nacional. (Comments received from Dr. Germán Sarmiento Palacio, Colombian lawyer.)

[33] See Carlos Diaz Alejandro, *Los Mecanismos de Control de Importaciones* (Bogotá, Colombia: Fundación para el Desarrollo, 1972).

[34] Francisco Thoumi, *La Utilizació de Capital Instalado en Colombia* (Bogotá, Colombia: Fundación para el Desarrollo, 1974).

[35] A detailed guide of administrative procedures is published by Price Waterhouse: *Information Guide for Doing Business in Colombia* (Bogotá, Colombia: Price Waterhouse, May 1973). See also *Tax and Trade Guide, Colombia* (Chicago: Arthur Andersen and Co., Subject File AA702L, Item I, 1972).

With the new law, three main grounds for criticizing the previous "laissez faire" attitude toward foreign investment disappeared. First, in requiring all foreign investors to register their foreign investments, and limiting profit remittance each year to 14 percent of the registered foreign investment, the law eliminated the possibility that a foreign concern could establish a Colombian company with an insignificant capital base, and then proceed to finance the local operations with loans obtained from Colombian credit sources. Second, by requiring all contracts covering license agreements for the use of trademarks, patents, and know-how (which call for remittance abroad in foreign exchange) to be submitted and approved, the law effectively eliminated a "loophole" which had allowed international concerns to remit important sums abroad in the past. Third, as a step toward controlling price mark-ups in inter-company operations, the follow-up Decree Law 691 of 1967 created a special division of the Institute of Foreign Commerce (INCOMEX) to investigate the possible discrepancies between the international price and the inter-company price.[36]

It is important to note that this system obliges foreign investors to adjust their plans to the socioeconomic context of the country and it controls the inflow and outflow of capital and of technology. On the other hand, these control operations have a cost, and there is a lack of centralized institutions for negotiations with foreign investors.[37]

The consequences of the system of control. Within the new institutional framework, Colombia created a special division of the planning board to control foreign investment. The division has established a method for evaluating the costs and benefits of foreign investment, and this method has been approved by the highest ministerial commission on economic affairs, the National Council of Political Economy. The criteria used to screen foreign investment proposals are listed here in order of importance:

(1) the net effect on the balance of payments,

(2) the contribution to the improvement of the level of employment of the country,

(3) the technical complexity of the project and the use of national input,

---

[36] In fact, inter-company operations, especially transfer pricing practices, were not subject to specific controls. This point has been well developed by Constantine Vaitsos, *Transfer of Resources and Monopoly Rents*, Harvard Development Advisory Service, Economic Report No. 168, prepared for the Harvard Development Advisory Service Conference, Dubrovnik, 1970 (Cambridge, Mass.: The Center for International Affairs, Harvard University, 1970).

[37] Lombard, "Methodology," Chapter V.

Table 1

FRAMEWORK OF ANALYSIS OF A FOREIGN
INVESTMENT PROPOSAL ACCORDING TO
THE COLOMBIAN PLANNING BOARD

Background Information
    —Description of the project
    —Description of the nature of the investor

Justification of the Project According to the Investor

Evaluation of the Project
(1) Analysis of the balance of payments effect

    Positive effects:
        —Initial investment
        —Exports
        —Import substitution
        —Foreign loans

    Negative effects:
        —Imports
        —Profit repatriation on the basis of 14 percent of registered capital
        —Royalty payments
        —Amortization of capital
        —Foreign loan amortization
(2) Sectorial analysis
(3) Employment created
(4) Other factors

Qualitative Analysis of the Investment Project

Conclusion

Recommendation
(1) To approve or to improve
(2) The condition of approvals or reason for rejections

Source: Lombard, "Methodology," p. 301.

    (4) the participation of local capital within the venture,

    (5) the improvement of competition within the Colombian market, and

    (6) the impact of the project on Latin American integration.

The method used is shown in Table 1.[38]

    During the period after the promulgation of Decree Law 444, foreign investment proposals increased regularly (see Table 2), from

---

[38] Ibid., Chapter VII.

Table 2

FOREIGN INVESTMENT APPROVED IN COLOMBIA, 1967–74

(current U.S. $, in millions)

Year	Amount
1967	18.4
1968	20.0
1969	27.4
1970	38.9[a]
1971	32.9[b]
1972	16.8
1973	60.9
1974	120.0

[a] Including the Cerro Matoso Project of $29.2 million (U.S.).

[b] Including the Monomero-Colombo-Venezolano Project of $7.4 million (U.S.).

Sources: 1967-1969 data are from Document Number 436, *Información sobre la Inversión Privada Extranjera en Colombia* (Bogotá, Colombia: Departamento Nacional de Planeación, January 20, 1970); 1970-1974 figures are from *El Tiempo*, "Planeación Aprueba Inversión," February 3, 1974.

$18 million (U.S.) in 1967 to $38.9 million (U.S.) in 1970. These figures do, however, include one or two unusually large projects such as the Hanna Mining Project in Cerro Matoso. Nevertheless, they show that, in the Colombian case, the establishment of clear rules to control foreign investments did not absolutely deter capital investment: in fact, the amount of foreign investment increased after 1972 when the new rules were in effect.

At the same time, the Colombian planning board evaluated some of the activities of foreign firms. One of the most interesting studies was conducted by Constantine Vaitsos for the Colombian planning board and the Superintendency of Foreign Trade (INCOMEX). Analyzing in detail a sample of 117 contracts—87 in the pharmaceutical industry, 18 in the chemical sector, and 12 in the textile industry—Vaitsos found some kinds of clauses in the contracts for technology transfer between parent and subsidiary that were designed to preserve the monopoly rents of the parent corporations. These included:

(1) tie-in clauses for intermediate product purchases,

(2) tie-in clauses for machinery purchases,

(3) export restrictive clauses,

(4) tie-in clauses on personnel, and

(5) sale clauses.

The effect of these clauses was that the parent might "overprice" its goods and therefore export both earnings and tax receipts to the home country.

Vaitsos suggested prohibiting this policy of restrictive business practice within the Andean subregion. As he stated:

> The industrial countries, having realized the monopoly implications and the restrictive business practices that result from tie-in clauses have explicitly legislated against them. For example, tie-in clauses are contrary to the principles of Section 1 of the Sherman Act and Section 3 of the Clayton Act of the United States. The Justice Department and the Federal Trade Commission have exercised enforcement of these statutes. Developing countries have still to show in their legal system an awareness and control of the economic implications resulting from tie-in arrangements.[39]

This is part of the background for Article 20 of Decision 24 of the Andean Pact prohibiting tie-in clauses.

Not infrequently there were cases in which the seller rather than the buyer did most of the "questioning" and investigation during technology transfer.[40] The conclusion would be that the buyer was often buying a technology that had been published and could have been obtained for nearly nothing. Vaitsos suggested the creation of a subregional information center on technology and the development of a local technology. This is proposed in Article 54 of the Andean Pact.

In addition, the host-country policy might foster sub-optimal allocation of resources because the level of protection was too high. To limit dividend repatriation without adequate pricing controls would be an incentive to export tax receipts through transfer pricing. Vaitsos recommended the implementation of adequate controls, including control over international price and economic policy, in order to diminish the firm's protection.

Common Regional Treatment of Foreign Capital: Decision 24. Lest this part of the chapter be considered a digression, it should be noted that we are discussing Decision 24 of the Andean Pact because it represents the basic norm for the selection and treatment of foreign investment in Colombia, as well as because the importance of Colombian efforts in the adoption of Decision 24 underscores the impor-

---

[39] Vaitsos, *Transfer of Resources*, pp. 15-16.
[40] Ibid., p. 17.

tance of Colombia as an exemplar of Third World problems and solutions.

Colombia's contribution to the adoption of Decision 24. In 1966 the president of Colombia, Dr. Carlos Lleras Restrepo, in concert with President Frei of Chile, organized a summit meeting in Bogotá where it was decided to promote the integration of a special Andean Common Market. The two presidents recommended a subregional agreement of transitional character with internal tariff structures within the context of the Latin American Free Trade Association (LAFTA). A special role was given to foreign investment.

> We think that private foreign capital can make a substantial contribution to the economic development of Latin America, so long as it stimulates the capitalization of the countries in which it locates and facilitates a broad participation of national capital in that process.[41]

The Cartagena Agreement was signed on June 3, 1969. Following the recommendations of P. Rosenstein Rodan, the six Andean countries [42] decided to draft a common treatment of foreign capital. The Colombian representatives suggested the following points:

First, the balance of payments effects of foreign investment should be studied in detail. Foreign investors should not be allowed to repatriate more than a set percentage of earnings or of their registered capital. Colombia indicated that 14 percent was a figure that had been used with success, and the now well-known 14 percent limit on profit repatriation was thus adopted under the suggestion of the Colombian representative. It may be noted that, if a foreign investor contributes substantially to the balance of payments of a country, especially by exporting more than 80 percent of his production, he will be subject to a more favorable profit repatriation rate.

Second, restrictive business practices, especially those linked with technology transfer, should be controlled and indeed avoided. These recommendations were based on the Colombian research on transfer pricing done by Constantine Vaitsos and presented at a regional seminar on technology transfer held in Bogotá in 1970.[43]

---

[41] Declaración de Bogotá in *Historia Documental del Acuerdo de Cartagena* (Lima, Peru, 1974), p. 222.

[42] Bolivia, Chile, Colombia, Ecuador, Peru, and Venezuela.

[43] Miguel S. Wionczek, *Inversión y Tecnología Extranjera en América Latina* (Mexico City: Cuadernos de Joaquín Mortiz, 1971), p. 71.

This basis explains the careful study of technology contracts required by Articles 18 to 25 of Decision 24. Moreover, Decision 24 instituted a royalty committee in each country similar to the one in Colombia and created a regional center of information on available technology.

Third and fourth, foreign firms should contribute to developing the local capital markets and should sell their stock locally, and national governments should be given an escape clause for granting exceptions in a given sector of the economy if they think it necessary (Article 44 of Decision 24).

Clauses suggested by other countries. It is clear that the governments of Chile and Peru were specifically concerned about the political costs of foreign investment and the role of government-owned enterprise. These countries insisted on the objective of avoiding all "dependencia" toward U.S. and European multinational corporations, and on establishing a mechanism to control foreign companies. This is the fade-out process (or divestment phase) previously suggested by such writers as Hirschman [44] and Rosenstein Rodan.[45]

The general idea of the "divestment phase" is that within fifteen years national investors will have majority ownership in all the companies that want to take advantage of the Andean market. The influence of the national investor should be reflected in the management of the company. Also, foreign investors should be excluded from key sectors of the economy in order to preserve the host country's independence. The key sectors from which foreign investors should be excluded are basic industries (Article 38 of Decision 24), insurance and banking (Article 42), transportation and advertising (Article 43), broadcasting and public utilities (Article 41), and all sectors already adequately served (Article 38). Moreover, a preference should be given to state-owned enterprises over privately owned enterprises.[46]

---

[44] A. O. Hirschman, *How to Divest in Latin America and Why*, Princeton Essays in International Finance (Princeton: Princeton University Press, 1969).

[45] Paul Rosenstein Rodan, *Multinational Investment in the Framework of Latin American Integration* (Washington, D. C.: Inter-American Development Bank, 1968), p. 35.

[46] For Mejia Palacio, a high executive in a Colombian Bank, this is one of the "political elements" appearing in the Decision 24. A foreign investor, who would make an agreement with the state, would be given two advantages: first, the investor's joint-venture would in certain cases be considered as a "mixed" enterprise and be given the advantages of the Andean market (Article 36, Andean Pact), and second, the investor might obtain a guarantee or voucher from the state for obtaining financial credit (Article 15, Andean Pact).

Decision 24 was finally integrated into Colombian Law by Decree 1900 of September 15, 1973.[47] It is now the norm for the treatment of foreign investment in Colombia. It aims at giving increased bargaining power to each of the Andean countries, and constitutes a "new phase in the quest for a normative order regarding direct foreign investment," to quote Covey T. Oliver, former U.S. Ambassador to Colombia.[48] Because it is a minimal norm, Colombia has supplemented Decision 24 by other specific measures.

Measures taken by Colombia to supplement Decision 24. Colombia in recent years (1973–1975) has supplemented Decision 24 by a series of specific decisions:

First, a minority joint-venture (one in which Colombians own a majority of the stock) is welcome and will be treated as a national firm and obtain an immediate approval of the planning board. This is in some respects an extension of the clause indicating that foreign firms should disclose their divestment plans if they want to take advantage of the enlarged regional market.

Second, all new investment that involves the creation of a physical plant should be located outside the major cities (Bogotá, Medellín, Barranquilla, and Cali). In other words, foreign investment will be one tool of the decentralization policy. Exempted from this requirement are firms exporting more than 80 percent of their production, and nonpolluting small and medium-sized firms. (The effect of all firms on pollution will be carefully studied.)

Third, some sectors were given preferential treatment. The petroleum industry is subject to a special regulation concerning its mode of exploitation, its pricing practices, and its foreign exchange possibilities. (This special regulation is based on the priority given by the government to developing its energy base and raw materials.) In the mining sector, joint ventures are recommended as second best, the best being technology contracts. Foreign firms are granted a special possibility for profit remittances. In the tourist industry, national participation should be at least 15 percent from the begin-

---

[47] For the details of the legal controversy, see the excellent legal analysis by José Joaquín Caicedo, "La Incorporación de las Decisiones 24 y 34 al Derecho Colombiano," *Revista Cámara de Comercio de Bogotá*, vol. 3, no. 11 (June 1973).

[48] C. T. Oliver, "The Andean Foreign Investment Code: A New Phase in the Quest for Normative Order as to Foreign Investment," in *American Journal of International Law*, vol. 3, no. 5 (1972), pp. 763-784. For a useful guide for adapting to recent legislative changes, see Susan S. Holland and Esteban A. Ferrer, eds., *Changing Legal Environment in Latin America: Management Implications*, vol. 1: *Argentina, Brazil, Colombia, México, Venezuela* (New York: Council of the Americas, 1974).

ning, but foreign investors do not have to convert to "mixed" enterprises. The foreign companies of the internal commerce sector (marketing and distribution) will be authorized to increase their capital if they export 40 percent of their sales or diversify the present trade.

Finally, it may be noted that from 1970 to 1974 the Colombian attitude toward the banking sector was quite flexible, but that this attitude has recently changed drastically (which is the subject of this study). According to Decree 295, foreign banks must convert themselves into joint ventures called "mixed" companies. Various issues remain unclear. How will the foreign firms value their stocks? Will they find local buyers? Will they convert themselves into minority joint ventures, or leave the country? One of the first sectors that must adapt to the new norm will be the foreign banks. Their adaptation may create a precedent for other sectors in Colombia, and in other Latin American countries as well.

2. FOREIGN BANKS IN COLOMBIA

Foreign bank assets represent about 10 percent of the total assets of commercial banks in Colombia, and the foreign banks control an important part of external loans both to the private and to the public sector. Overall, we have concluded that the foreign banks control 34 percent of the Colombian banking sector, including external loans,[49] but we admit that any figure is open to discussion. At the outset, before we can analyze the current situation, we should know when foreign banks came to Colombia, and why, what their importance has been, and how they have been treated.

The History of Foreign Banking in Colombia. The relation between Colombia and the international financial market is quite old. England as well as France loaned money to Colombia during the War of Independence. In 1913, a century after the beginnings of the Latin American wars for independence, French investments in government bonds of Latin American countries amounted to $987 million (U.S.), and in private direct investments to $586 million (U.S.). The first foreign banks that succeeded in staying in Colombia were the Bank of London and Montreal, which came in 1920, the French and Italian

---

[49] François Lombard, "Perspectivas de la Colombianización de los Bancos Extranjeros: Oportunidades y Problemas," mimeographed (Bogotá, Colombia: Universidad de los Andes, 1975).

Bank for Latin America, which came in 1924, and the Royal Bank of Canada, which came in 1925.[50]

The first U.S. bank in Colombia was the First National City Bank (Citibank), which set up a branch in 1929. In the words of E. Taylor Parks:

> In 1930, a loan of 20,000,000 US dollars was promised by the First National City Bank to the Colombian government on the following conditions: a balanced budget, the flotation of an internal loan of 6,000,000 million pesos and a reform of the financial and customs systems. Sufficient reform progress was soon made for the advance of 3,000,000 dollars. In October, some 9,000,000 dollars more were released.[51]

In recent years, two other U.S. banks have come to Colombia. In 1966, the Bank of America started its operations there. (This late arrival may be explained by the fact that the Bank of America had been able to have branch banks throughout the whole state of California, whereas some of its competitors—such as the First National City Bank—were authorized to have domestic branches only in New York City and contiguous counties within New York state, and therefore expanded overseas.) In 1967, the Chase Manhattan Bank took a minority (but substantial) participation in the Banco del Comercio (43 percent with the Deutsche Sudamerikanische Bank taking 5 percent).[52]

The growth of the U.S. banking in Colombia may be correlated with the growth of the U.S. manufacturing investment there in recent years. U.S. firms investing in Colombia required services that were not available locally, and hence may reasonably have suggested that their home banks extend a network of branches on a worldwide basis. In any case, the main growth of foreign banking in Colombia came during the 1960s. Of seven foreign banks there now, three came in this period: Banque Nationale pour le Commerce et l'Industrie (BNCI), Bank of America, and Chase Manhattan Bank. Figures 2 and 3 reflect the comparative importance of U.S. and European banks in Colombia during this period.

The growth of U.S. banks in Colombia may be explained by at least three factors: their client base, their loan strategies, and their personnel strategies. Citibank, Bank of America, and Chase Man-

---

[50] United Nations, *El Financiamiento Externo de América Latina* (New York: United Nations, 1964).

[51] Parks, *Colombia and the United States*, p. 474.

[52] H. Melo, *Algunos Aspectos de las Relaciones entre los Grupos Locales y el Capital Extranjero en Colombia*, mimeographed (Bogotá, Colombia: Universidad Nacional de Colombia, 1974).

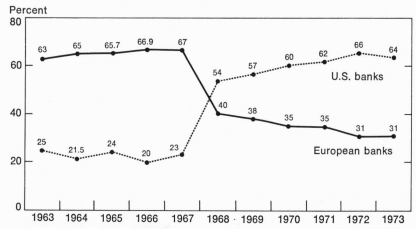

Figure 2

PERCENTAGE OF TOTAL FOREIGN BANK ASSETS HELD BY U.S. AND EUROPEAN BANKS IN COLOMBIA, 1963–1973

Note: European banks included are Banco Frances e Italiano, Banco Franco-Colombiano, and Banco de Londres y Montreal. U.S. banks included are First National City Bank, Bank of America, and Banco del Comercio (43 percent owned by Chase Manhattan).

Source: *Revista de la Superintendencia Bancaria* (Bogotá, Colombia), February issues from 1964 to 1974. Calculations by François Lombard.

Figure 3

ASSETS OF A TYPICAL U.S. AND TYPICAL EUROPEAN BANK, 1964–1973

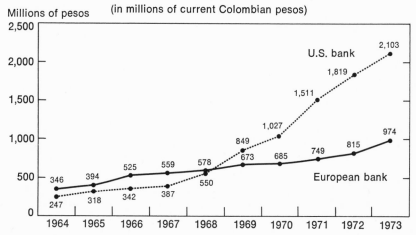

Source: Same as Figure 2.

hattan serve the multinational corporations. As stated in Citibank's *Annual Report:*

> Our company has anticipated the growth of the multi-national corporation and is now positioned to make the most of the opportunities that our international clients create. We have a comprehensive ability to serve the special needs of our multinational customer which we call "world corporations." Typically, our multinational customer has 15 subsidiaries and affiliates that bank with us in 11 countries, though some of the biggest have relationships with our branches in over 30 countries.[53]

Such U.S. multinational corporations as International Business Machines, General Electric, Xerox, and Exxon (Esso Inter-America), operate in Colombia. These growing corporations would normally choose to do business with a U.S. bank with which they were already doing business in other countries. That in part explains why there is a strong correlation between the growth and success of U.S. firms in Colombia and the expansion there of U.S. banks that offer standard services around the world. There are definite reasons for a "world corporation" to do business with a "world bank."

Moreover, the policy of the U.S. banks has been innovative and aggressive. A company such as Citibank offers an extensive range of services: personal services which are normally carried out rapidly and well, consumer finance, leasing, export financing, and international syndication in the Eurodollar markets. In many of these areas, Citibank was the first bank in Colombia to offer the services, in part because of its technological resources, in part because of its ability to take risks.

One of the reasons for the aggressiveness of U.S. firms lies in personnel and organizational structures. In a U.S. bank, there are training programs that each new employee receives. An example is the First National City Bank's training program:

> The objective of this program is to fulfill the needs of managers and credit analysts of FNCB expanding organization. The training program lasts four months and a half. During the first two months, trainees are full time in training: the mornings are spent in the credit training program and the afternoons in operations training program. After this period, participants are assigned as credit assistants to one of the Bogotá marketing groups. By this time, they are fully conversant in financial language (accounting), adept at interpreting a financial statement (financial analysis), aware of

---

[53] Citicorp, *1972 Annual Report* (New York: Citicorp, 1973), p. 12.

the theory of our credit procedures (credit policy), and knowledgeable of how a credit presentation is made (credit policy).[54]

Citibank currently employs 800 persons in Colombia and is training 30 persons a year. The Citibank employees generally are given rapid promotions. The age level of officers is around thirty-two to thirty-five, whereas in other banks the age level of the officers is much higher—say forty to fifty years. The turnover in employees of U.S. banks is quite high, suggesting that a real transfer of technology may take place in these banks, to the social benefit of Colombia.

Another consequence of the growth of the U.S. banks is, however, that these banks have been perceived as a threat to local banks. The local banks fear losing some of their best employees, who might like an increase in salary and the opportunities provided by a multinational corporation. Moreover, the local banks might lose their peso deposits because some clients would prefer the fast and numerous services, or the prestige, of an international bank.

The Importance of Foreign Banks in the Colombian Banking Sector. There are various ways of measuring the importance of foreign banks in a given country: earnings, repatriated earnings, assets, capital. We have selected assets on the books as our index, even though some assets may be undervalued. At least assets, as an index, combine outstanding loans and invested capital. Nevertheless, one must be aware that the assets on the Colombian books do not necessarily give an accurate overall picture. This question is discussed below (pp. 27–28).

Another way of measuring the importance of foreign banks would be to evaluate their participation in Colombian banks. There is a strong interaction between local and international banks, as is indicated in Figure 4. The funds controlled by foreign banks may take the form of the assets of the foreign banks in local currency, of outstanding external loans granted by headquarters to the private and public sectors, and of the participation of the foreign banks in local banks.

The best source of information on the balance sheets of the subsidiaries of foreign banks in local pesos is the *Revista* of the Banking Superintendency. The information is in the public domain, and

---

[54] Federico Ochoa, *Colcad-Credit Training Program* (Bogotá, Colombia: First National City Bank, September 1974).

Figure 4
INTERACTION BETWEEN LOCAL AND INTERNATIONAL BANKS

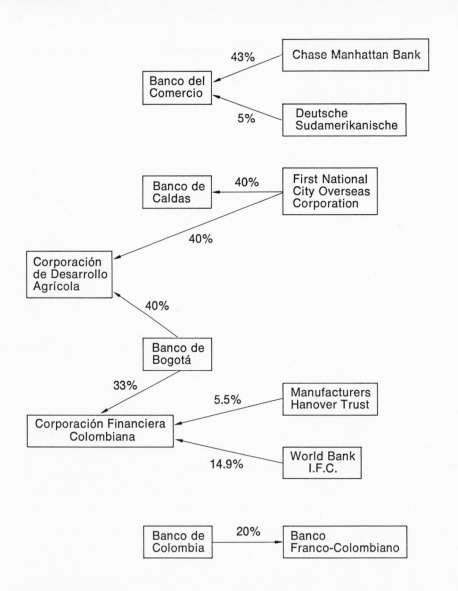

Source: H. Melo, *Observaciones sobre el Papel del Capital Extranjero y sus Relaciones con los Grupos Locales de Colombia* (Bogotá, Colombia: Centro de Investigación para el Desarrollo, Universidad Nacional de Colombia, 1974), and personal research of the authors.

most economists interested in the topic have analyzed it. The results show the importance of the outstanding loans and deposits controlled by the foreign banks in Colombia. The data are given schematic form in Figures 5 and 6. These data may be said to measure the "surface" importance of foreign banks in Colombia. For 1973, the assets of foreign banks amounted to 13.6 percent of the assets of all commercial banks and generated 9.7 percent of the earnings of the entire Colombian banking sector. This importance is not overwhelming.

On the other hand, the parent (or home office) foreign banks may offer, within the Colombian legal framework, external loans in dollars, and these are an important part of an "iceberg." These loans involve credit facilities for improving machinery and other capital goods of national and social interest.[55] If the loans are granted by the home offices in San Francisco, New York, or Paris, they need not legally appear on the books in Colombia and are called "off book" operations. There are several difficulties in keeping track of these loans.

First, as the number of loans approved is very high (up to 7,000 for 1973), it is hard to categorize them according to lending entities. This categorization has not yet been carried out by the Colombian authorities, and Colombia has therefore no way of knowing which banks are lending to whom. A second problem involves the indirect loans. A U.S. bank may lend to the headquarters of a U.S. multinational corporation with some kind of special mortgage provision. The loan may be transferred from the home office to the subsidiary in Colombia, and the mortgage will be placed on the property in Colombia. Officially this loan is an inter-company loan, but it may actually be a loan from (say) Marine Midland Trust to (say) the Hotel Latinia in Cartagena. A last item generally not considered is made up of the loans made available by the private sector to the Colombian government and to the public sector including private firms with governmental guarantees. Using all available figures for private dollar loans, we have arrived at a financial dependence index of 34 percent including private internal and external loans.[56]

This information is presented in Tables 3 and 4. The public sector in Colombia has increased its indebtedness to the private international money market because of the availability of funds from international banks in the early 1970s. There has come to be a high

---

[55] See, for instance, Article 128 of Decree 444 of March 1967, *Official Gazette*, Republic of Colombia.

[56] See Lombard, "Methodology," Chapter 9, and Carlos Caballero Argaez, "La Colombianización Financiera," *El Tiempo*, May 23, 1975, pp. 5A, 7A.

Figure 5

IMPORTANCE OF FOREIGN BANKS MEASURED BY SHARE OF COLOMBIAN COMMERCIAL BANK ASSETS, 1963–1973

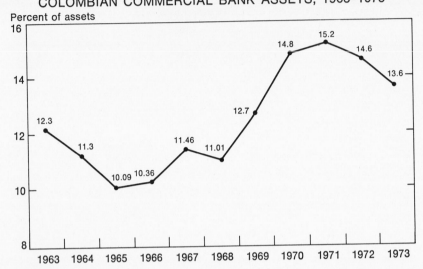

Percent of assets

Source: *Revista de la Superintendencia Bancaria* (Bogotá, Colombia), various issues. Calculation ours.

Figure 6

IMPORTANCE OF FOREIGN BANKS MEASURED BY SHARE OF COLOMBIAN BANKING SECTOR EARNINGS, 1963–1973

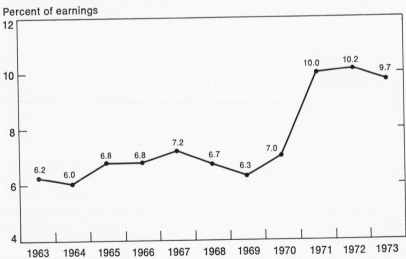

Percent of earnings

Source: Same as in Figure 5.

Table 3

LOANS BY FOREIGN BANKS TO THE PUBLIC SECTOR IN COLOMBIA, 1968–73

(current U.S. $, in thousands)

Entities	1968	1969	1970	1971	1972	1973
National government	$ 5,200	$ 7,924	$ 6,917	$ 9,785	$ 91,433	$134,731
Decentralized institutions	6,712	8,239	7,299	18,955	25,354	50,191
Departments	1,607	539	90	—	—	—
County institutions	—	30	250	250	994	829
Private entity with governmental guarantee	450	893	4,714	10,992	10,540	17,719
Bank of the Republic	19,414	10,242	3,500	10,000	8,000	6,000
Total	$33,383	$27,867	$22,770	$50,073	$136,321	$209,470

Source: Data obtained from personal interviews at foreign banks.

Colombian debt level, with foreign banks established in Colombia controlling up to 41 percent of the funds available (funds including the assets of commercial banks in pesos and private external loans to Colombia). This figure may be misleadingly high in the sense that some foreign loans do not involve any control by an international bank. The role of the international bank in these loans is merely to present the bond issues and float them.

What we can say for certain is that, in Colombia, the visible part of the activities of foreign banks represents 14 percent of all banking activity, and this part is controllable by the government, especially by the Monetary Board and the Banking Superintendency. The other part of the "iceberg"—the remaining 20 percent or 30 percent—is not controllable directly: this part represents the business of foreign banks that have representatives in the country rather than an investment in branches. It may be noted that the government, by fostering public loans, may contribute to the growth of foreign banks in the country.

With the growth of the so-called financial dependence on foreigners, partly from the lack of internal funds, partly from foreign exchange, and partly from the range of the services offered, Colombia has grown concerned over the role of foreign commercial banks and has tried to curtail that role.

Table 4

LOANS BY SELECTED PRIVATE BANKS
TO THE PUBLIC SECTOR IN COLOMBIA, 1968–73

(current U.S. $, in thousands)

Banks	1968	1969	1970	1971	1972	1973
Chase Manhattan Bank	—	—	—	2,119	42,119	43,612
First National City Bank	—	—	1,000	10,750	8,000	6,375
Bank of London	3,426	2,738	1,186	3,386	7,018	25,000
Dillon Read [a]	—	—	—	—	—	60,000 [a]
Bank of America	5,200	7,924	6,924	4,523	—	—
French Bank Consortium	—	—	170	9,095	14,174	16,270
Manufacturers Hanover	1,000	3,555	2,666	6,070	44,270	7,391

[a] Group of banks including Chemical Bank—$20,000, United California—$10,000, and Industrial Bank of Japan—$14,000 (dollars in thousands).
Source: Same as Table 3.

The Legal Treatment of Foreign Banks in Colombia. The foreign banks in Colombia as well as the Colombian banks are supervised by the Banking Superintendency (Superintendencia Bancaria), which determines whether the banks are complying with the norms established by the Monetary Board and the Ministry of Finance. The Monetary Board regulates the growth of the money supply, the lending policy—in brief, Colombian monetary policy. The difference in treatment of the foreign banks and the domestic banks is that the foreign banks are subject to the norms affecting all foreign investments.

During the period from 1967 to 1973, the foreign banks were in essence subject to the requirements of Decree 444. When these banks wanted to increase their capital base in Colombia, they had to obtain the approval of the planning board, and in specific cases, of the National Council of Political Economy. After 1973, they were subject to Decision 24 of the Andean Pact.

In 1969, the planning board and the Colombian government (then under the Liberal Carlos Lleras Restrepo) made a detailed analysis of their stance toward foreign banks and suggested a highly restrictive policy. They noted that two arguments

have been expressed to justify the presence of foreign banks in the country: the necessity of bringing new savings to this economic sector, and the importance played by these institutions as a channel to attract foreign investments and external credit to our country. To each of these arguments, there is an alternative response: internal savings can be created by adequate mechanisms, and the representatives of foreign banks can play the same role as foreign subsidiaries in attracting foreign investments.[57]

In particular, the policy recommended did not permit the capital increase of existing banks or the entry of new banks. This would have gradually reduced the importance of foreign banks in Colombia. But the Conservative party that came into power in 1970 was more favorable to foreign banks—indeed more favorable to foreign investors—than the Liberals. In 1971, the newspaper, El Siglo, controlled by Senator Alvaro H. Caicedo (Conservative), noted that, "We are against the new restricted status of foreign capital. The problem of the country is not the excessive dependence on the foreigners, but to foster the economic growth and investment. With the small level of savings that we generate, it is not possible to accelerate economic growth."[58] This point of view was also expressed by the finance minister, Rodrigo Llorente: "Foreign banks have achieved an important mission not only for their capital inflow, but because they are one of the best means to promote healthy investments and to show outside the true economic situation of the country."[59]

Public opinion in part and many industrialists supported foreign investors. When the ratification of Decision 24 was under study by the Second Commission of the Senate in preparation for Law 8 of May 1973, considerable "give and take" took place between the industrial group and the government. Decision 24 would be ratified, but an exemption would be given to foreign investors in the mining, internal commercial, and banking sectors.[60] The result was a growth of foreign investment in the banking sector as described in Figures 7 and 8. The investments in the financial sector represented 28 percent to 30 percent of the investments approved by the planning board in

---

[57] These arguments appeared in *Las Inversiones Extranjeras en el Sector Financiero Colombiano—Recomendaciones de una Política*, Colombian Planning Board, Department of Industrial and Agricultural Studies, Working Paper No. 297 (Bogotá, 1969).

[58] *El Siglo*, November 11, 1971.

[59] *El Tiempo*, November 4, 1971.

[60] For more detail, see the description of the events of this period in John Carlsen and Peter Neers, *Peru's and Colombia's Policies on Foreign Technology* (Copenhagen, Denmark: Institute for Development Research, May 1974); Wionczek, *Inversión y Tecnología Extranjera*, p. 131, and same in *Comercio Exterior*, June 1971.

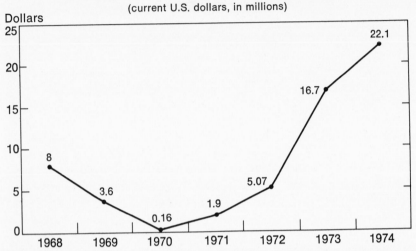

Figure 7

INVESTMENT IN THE FINANCIAL SECTOR APPROVED BY
COLOMBIAN PLANNING BOARD, 1968–1974

(current U.S. dollars, in millions)

Sources: *Información sobre la Inversión Extranjera en Colombia,* Departamento Nacional de Planeación, Working Paper No. 678, by Unidad de Estudios Industriales y Agrícolas, December 9, 1970. *Solicitudes de Inversión Extranjera Aprobadas por el Departamento Nacional de Planeación en 1969, 1970, 1971, 1972 y 1973* (mimeographed).

Figure 8

FOREIGN FINANCIAL SECTOR INVESTMENT AS A
PERCENTAGE OF TOTAL INVESTMENT APPROVED, 1969–1974

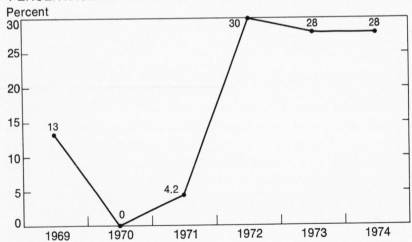

Sources: Same as Figure 7.

1972, 1973, and 1974. The foreign investments in the financial sector approved during the period from 1970 through 1974 involved leasing, export promotion, and consumer finance companies.

In December 1973, Colombia passed Decrees 2791 and 2788, which exempted foreign banks from the Andean Statute of Capital.[61] A Decree 387 of March 7, 1974, required that all new investment in the financial sector be authorized by the National Council of Political Economy with prior approval of the Banking Superintendency. The foreign banking sector in Colombia was relieved. Instead of being required to convert themselves into national banks and to sell 80 percent of their stock, they would be free to operate in the country without considering conversion.

The situation of foreign banks in Colombia seemed to have been resolved when, after a series of studies at various governmental institutions, the newly elected Liberal party government prepared a law requiring that foreign banks be converted to "mixed" enterprises. This law was not initially presented to the Colombian Congress for a series of legal and political reasons, but on February 24, 1975, Decree 295 signed by the president and the minister of finance created "a Commission to arrange the transformation of foreign banks and the other institutions into 'mixed' enterprises."[62] The commission was given legal power to achieve this transformation[63] and was empowered to prepare proposed laws and regulations on this issue.[64] The timing of this decree was a surprise to the foreign banks.

This Decree 295 evidently represents a key element in the Colombian policy toward foreign investment. It can be precedent-setting in the sense that, as Colombia handles this fade-out process, so other Latin American (and indeed other Third World) countries may act.

3. PERCEPTIONS OF THE ISSUES

This section sets out the results of our survey on the views taken toward Decree 295. Because the issues raised are both recent and important, the survey took the form of personal interviews, rather than relying either on published opinion or on written questionnaires.

---

[61] For the sake of clarity, we have not mentioned the various legal norms dealing with foreign banks cancelled by the Supreme Court of Justice, such as the Articles 58, 59, 60 and 61 of the Decree 2153 of November 5, 1971, which regulated Decision 24 of the Andean Pact.

[62] Article 1.

[63] Article 2.

[64] Article 3.

The Survey Method. We conducted interviews with representatives of government, domestic banks, and foreign banks—the three entities most directly concerned with and knowledgeable about the potential impact and future prospects of Decree 295. Eight managers and technical experts from the government were interviewed, eight from domestic banks, and twenty-six from foreign banks.[65]

The contents of this chapter are based on these interviews, conducted mainly in June 1975. Our objective has been to reflect as faithfully and clearly as possible the variations within and among these three points of view so that the reader can have an accurate digest of the relevant interview information. Some quotations are given to illustrate the points and to provide a more realistic flavor or "feel" to the narrative. The topics and issues covered in these semi-structured interviews are shown below by a series of questions. The issues came partly from the respondents themselves in earlier interviews. We have attempted in all cases not to identify individuals, but rather to focus on the perceptions which the respondent conveyed at the time. We are looking not at individuals but at the issues themselves.

These are the nine questions which will serve as an outline for reporting the interview responses:

(1) How important is Decree 295?
(2) What are the reasons for the decree?
(3) What are the government's long range goals?
(4) What are the possible effects of Decree 295?
(5) Are Colombian investors interested in buying the stock of the foreign banks?
(6) What are the problems of stock valuation?
(7) Is some additional mechanism needed to improve the dialogue between the government and the foreign banks?
(8) What are the most likely negotiating procedures?
(9) Can neutral observers play a useful role in this situation?

The Survey Findings. In what follows, we have organized our findings by question and then by point of view (government, domestic banks, foreign banks) within the question.

---

[65] These interviews were with key decision makers and other well-informed individuals: heads and representatives of foreign banks, heads of leading domestic banks, and appropriate government officials. Our sample was intended to be representative of the various viewpoints, the only exceptions being a few government officials who were reluctant to speak openly on the issues at this time. Some of the foreign bank representatives had been government officials previously.

How important is Decree 295? As one might expect, Decree 295 is viewed differently by the different parties involved, some with skepticism, some with wishful thinking, others with real political concern. For the government, the issue is viewed as being politically important at the internal and regional level, but as being of minor importance economically.

One of the accepted ground-rules of Decision 24 of the Andean Pact is that, in the sectors already adequately served, no foreign investment should be authorized. Moreover, the banking sector is explicitly recognized as a sector in which no new foreign enterprise should be authorized (Article 42). Various studies made by the Colombian planning board show the importance of foreign banks, with assets amounting to 20 to 25 percent of the assets of commercial banks, a figure differing from ours because of the method of calculation. The government believes that the growth of foreign banks has been a little excessive. As President Alfonso López Michelsen stated during his campaign for the presidency, "Colombia is a country where foreign investment has had, and should always have, a minor role."[66]

In passing the decree, the government acted (in its view) in accordance with the expectations of the millions of Colombians who believe they should control their own financial resources, especially in a sector not requiring sophisticated technology. Typical comments received were these:

> We think foreign banks have little justification because we believe that, in this sector, they bring very little. The raw material are the deposits which are in their totality Colombian. Their technology is nearly nonexistent because the national banks can offer the same services.[67]

> We have always thought that the Colombian financial sector was quite efficient, and we did not need foreigners in this field.

> Foreign banks control an important part of our resources, and we cannot effectively control their operations, which range from indirect loans to controlling participation in National Banks.

In relation to the other Andean countries, one comment was:

> Ecuador and Venezuela have restrictive regulations; we had to be in line with this regional policy.

---

[66] "The Candidates and the Chamber," *Colombian-American Business Review*, vol. 13 (July-September 1973), p. 31.

[67] Jorge Valencia Jaramillo, ex-minister, member of the Colombian Congress, "Los Bancos Extranjeros," *El Tiempo*, June 17, 1975.

Other views expressed were:

> The government is very serious about this measure. It is quite a religion for them.

> In my opinion the Colombianization of foreign banks is the most important measure taken recently by the government.

> This measure was suggested by the Ministry which is now the most solid after the recent Paris negotiations and it is important for them. It is a governmental issue backed by the Congress.

> If the banks are not converted soon, government will lose its prestige;[68] therefore it has to do it rapidly.

As we might expect, the domestic banks hold various conflicting views. Some consider this measure an undesirable one because of the risks of retaliation they may suffer in their operations abroad, and others think the local banks will benefit. One position was:

> There is one foreign bank which started the conversion process two years ago and our relationships with them have been quite positive. We think this measure was expected and is in line with the philosophy of Decision 24. It is an important measure for national banks and we back it up.

The opposite view was the following:

> National banks have no vested interest in promoting this latest measure. They consider it as inopportune and difficult to implement, especially at a moment when Colombian banks are planning to set up wholly owned branches abroad.

As one might expect, Decree 295 is viewed as an important issue by foreign banks since they probably will have to abide by it or leave the country. While this is not the unanimous view, this issue is considered important because (1) it requires a critical and difficult decision for the foreign banks involved, (2) it has precedent-setting implications for other Latin American countries, (3) it has precedent-setting implications worldwide, and (4) it is an example of the testing ground, or interface, between two worldwide forces.

Comments from foreign bankers illustrate these points:

> I see two main forces in the world on a collision course: (1) governments want more control of multinational corporations at a time when (2) multinationals strongly feel the need for more internal control due to the increasing complexity and uncertainties of the world environment. These two views will have to be reconciled because countries can-

---

[68] See, for instance, "Paralizada Negociación con Bancos Extranjeros," *El Tiempo,* May 31, 1975.

not drop out of the world economy, and companies need foreign markets.

The government wants us to agree [to convert to a "mixed" status] before we know what we're getting into, because there are no guidelines in writing from the government.

This bank has minority interests in other parts of the world, but has never changed from a wholly owned to a minority position.

The Colombian position could have a "domino effect" throughout Latin America.

This may be a worldwide trend in which local participation—either private or public—will be required.

Others indicated that, from Colombia's point of view, the decree does not represent a major problem:

This is not important because of the relatively small size of foreign bank investments in Colombia as compared with the total banking picture.

I am not sure if the Commission will generate a lengthy report that nobody will read and the issue will be forgotten, or if it is a serious decision. In this case, it will be hard for our bank which has been here for many years and which will have, in some sense, to leave the country.

Further insight on the importance of this decree is provided by responses on several other closely related issues. In any case, the importance of the issue is of course seen differently by each group. On one side, the government is pursuing a political objective, while the foreign banks see it as an economic decision affecting their home office policy and strategy. It is clear that the government wants to implement this decree rapidly because of the political importance of the issue.

What are the reasons for the recent banking decree? There are various explanations of the decree. Each party has its own version of the story. The reasons given by government officials are that (1) foreign banks have been quite important especially in the provision of external loans, (2) banking is a sector where technology is not critical, (3) it is a sector well attended to by domestic banks, and (4) other Andean countries have shown the way to set up a nationalistic flag in banking.

Two subsidiary questions should be cleared up. Why was the decree only passed in February 1975, and why did the government not propose a law to the Congress? The timing can be explained by the fact that the new Liberal government declared an "economic emergency" in September 1974, just a month after assuming office, and that it took time for the basic studies to be carried out and for the issue to be put on the agenda of the National Council of Political Economy (CONPES). The fact that government passed a decree creating a commission is understandable inasmuch as the president was given the power to establish decrees in accordance with Decision 24.[69] One comment received was that:

> We prepared a very strict decree requiring that foreign banks become "mixed" enterprises. This solution was not approved by the legal advisor of the president, who indicated that we might get an appeal from the lawyers of foreign banks. We had, therefore, to draft this decree which created an *ad hoc* commission in charge of obtaining a voluntarily negotiated and accepted conversion of foreign banks.

The government is fully aware that this decree does not have the force of a law, but it believes that the Congress will vote such a law. "Who could decently fight against it and defend publicly the interest of foreigners?" (Also the procedure followed was in line with the concept of dialogue or "concerted economy" that was suggested by some of the presidential advisors.)[70] Domestic banks are aware of the political reasons for the decree and claim not to be directly pushing for the decree. Foreign-bank managers seem to be aware of the reasons for the decree, even if some wonder about its "force of sanction" and its logic.

Many of the foreign-bank managers interviewed said the main reason for the decree was "political," although several said there did not seem to have been much public pressure on this particular issue. No one suggested an economic basis for the decree, and opinion was mixed as to whether some domestic banks and other potential investors had been pushing for the decree.

Some believed that, the government being a strong supporter of the Andean Pact, it was merely acting in a manner consistent with the pact's philosophy. It was also suggested that a 51 percent owner-

---

[69] The legal issue involved in Decree 295 of 1975 is this: By Law 8a of 1973 approving the Cartagena Agreement, the president had until December 31, 1973, special powers to implement Decision 24. By Decree 2719 of 1973, he exempted commercial banks and other financial institutions from the treatment of Article 42 of the Andean Pact and received special powers to regulate foreign banks (Article 4 of Decree 2719).

[70] See, for instance, the paper presented during the campaign of President López by Jaime Vidal Perdomo, Guillermo Perry, and Rafael Rivas Posada, *Algunas Ideas sobre el Mecanismo Institucional de la Concertación del Proceso de Planificación en Colombia* (Bogotá, Colombia: Universidad de Los Andes, November 1973).

ship does not necessarily mean absolute control of a firm if the shares are held by several owners. Examples of comments by different foreign-bank managers follow:

> The government wants to control all of the vital sectors of the economy, and banking is considered one of these.

> This decree is more political than economic: to show support and solidarity with Venezuela, and pressure from local investors who want to buy bank stock. It's an excellent, secure investment.

> I haven't observed any pressure from domestic banks for the decree.

> The government is not under public pressure regarding foreign banks; oil, for example, is much more so, at least potentially.

> The decree is not official; in fact, it is contrary to present law. It is an effort to bring about 51 percent local ownership without going to Congress to ask for a new law.

> The decree is not motivated by antagonism of the government or public. The public attitude here is better than in many other Latin American countries. The decree is felt to be right or desirable by government economists.

> Fifty-one percent of dispersed ownership does not necessarily result in control; even 80 percent might not if it is widely dispersed.

It appears clear from the various interviews that the legal subtlety of the decree has not been fully understood by some foreign-bank managers. The remark of one respondent—"The decree is not official; in fact it is contrary to present law. It is an effort to convert foreign banks without going to Congress"—is quite significant. The respondent mentions the weakness of the government's legal position without considering the government's administrative and political power. The administrative power is the discretionary power of the planning board to authorize or reject applications to increase the capital of foreign banks, among other things. The political power is the power of the Congress to pass a law more stringent and inflexible than Decree 295.

What are the government's long-range goals? Knowledge of long-range governmental goals is necessary for multinational corporations to be able to make political forecasts of the government's attitude toward foreign banks.

There is a general government policy toward foreign investment, though this policy is likely to be changed under certain conditions (such as the election of a Conservative president, if that should happen, in 1978), and the banking decree is in line with present (Liberal) policy. Some principles of current Colombian policy toward foreign investment have been publicly stated by President Alfonso López Michelsen and by the head of the planning board:

Colombia should have a selective policy toward foreign investment. It should not accept all kinds of foreign investment especially those which are of unilateral benefit for the country and the investor.[71]

Foreign investment which can be legally controlled should contribute to the objective of decentralization that Colombia is pursuing.[72]

As indicated by one high Colombian official, "The policy toward foreign investment is formulated not only in Colombia, but we must adjust our policy with that of our partners of the Andean Common Market; and the Commission of this organization is preparing some new regulations to implement Decision 24 more fully."

At the present stage, government officials are applying the principles previously stated, in a step toward implementing Decision 24 of the Andean Pact:

What the Commission, created by Decree 295, requires is the conversion of foreign banks into "mixed" enterprises. What is meant by a "mixed" enterprise is that the national participation in capital should be at least equal to 51 percent and should be reflected in the financial, personnel, legal and commercial administration of the firm.

At the present stage, we shoot for this 49-51 percent split of capital. We cannot tell if this will be forever, or if this will be reduced to 20 percent as normally required by the Andean Pact. It is a political decision depending on various factors: the fulfillment of a correct conversion into "mixed" enterprises, the situation of our international reserves, and the possible pressures exercised by our Andean partners.

Another government official stated:

I think foreign banks will have just to convert to "mixed" enterprises. We are aware of the contribution of foreign

---

71 President López's speech at the Colombo-American Chamber of Commerce, "The Candidates and the Chamber," *Colombian-American Business Review*, vol. 13 (July-September 1973), p. 31.

72 M. Urrutia's presentation of the plan in "Plan de Desarrollo con Enfasis en el Sector Rural," *El Tiempo*, June 5, 1975.

banks in training executives, promoting national exports, and we do not want to lose completely the contribution of the existing foreign banks.

The domestic banks could be concerned about the long-term goals of the government. Some observers formulated the hypothesis that the government is willing to nationalize all commercial banks and that it merely started with the foreign banks because they are an easy target. The views of three domestic bankers were:

The bank issue is part of a larger picture: fiscal reform, land reform, aiming at achieving a better income distribution in Colombia.

At the present stage, domestic banks are not in danger of nationalization.

This policy attempts to bring back national resources to national banks.

The position of foreign bankers is quite different. Considerable interest and concern are centered around the plans and goals of the Colombian government. Was this decree just a first step? What is going to be required next? Is this a test case? As Charles Kettering often said, "Everyone should be concerned about the future because we're going to spend the rest of our lives there."

Half the respondents believed the recent decree is likely to be just the first step, either for foreign banks or for other multinational firms. Roughly one quarter believed that the government may not have longer range goals but is only reacting to current events. And roughly one quarter believed this is not a first step but an end in itself.

Uncertainty about the future complicates the problem of making important decisions today. It also serves to create a climate lacking in confidence. Here is a sample of comments:

The big question mark is, what will the government require in the future? Is this a step toward even less ownership [by the foreign banks]?

Does the government have goals and future expectations toward which it's working?

The number one objective of this new government is to reduce inflation. Hence it has not used all the foreign money available in order to keep from adding to the money supply. This has resulted in a lowering of the government's financial reserves, but is only temporary. This is a transition period.

If the government were serious, it would ask for a change in the law to force the change.

The government says it welcomes foreign investment; however, the practice is not consistent with the stated policy.

This is a test case; other sectors expect to be hit next, and soon.

The recent decree is as far as the government wants to go.

The key question is, what does the government see as the role of the private banks in Colombia?

On this issue, it is interesting to note the contrast between the views of government officials and the views of the foreign bankers. Some foreign bankers, if we have understood them, said "foreign investment is supposedly welcome in Colombia," while the administration was saying clearly: "We will accept foreign investment only in the sectors where we think it is needed: mining, petroleum, tourism, and export promotion." Foreign investors apparently have had some difficulties in getting the message, perhaps as a result of misinformation or simply from a lack of communication. Meanwhile, let us see how the various groups viewed the impact of this decree.

What are the possible effects of Decree 295? In game theory or in bargaining situations, answering a question of this sort for each party is necessary in order to establish the pay-off matrix, based on a perception of the utility of each outcome.[73]

For government officials, various points must be considered: the most likely reaction of foreign banks, the macro-effects on the economy and the capital market, the micro-effects on the structure of the banking industry, and the external effects.

As one of the major international banks, Banque Nationale de Paris, has freely converted itself; we think it is possible and feasible for most of the other banks.

The macro-effects on the economy were judged minimal:

Foreign banks have a registered capital of about 40 million dollars. Even if they repatriate all their capital, if it is spread over five to ten years, the effect will be minimal on the balance of payments. Moreover this will reduce the future foreign exchange outflow of profit remittances.

---

[73] For more details on negotiation strategy, see Jack Sawyer and Harold Guetzkow, "Bargaining and Negotiations in International Relations," in Herbert C. Kelman, *International Behavior: A Socio-Psychological Analysis* (New York: Holt, 1965); Roger Fisher, *Conflict Resolution for Beginners* (New York: Harper and Row, 1969); T. C. Schelling, *The Strategy of Conflict* (Cambridge, Mass.: Harvard University Press, 1960); Karl Deutsch, *The Analysis of International Relations* (Englewood Cliffs, N.J.: Prentice Hall, 1968); and A. Kapoor, *Planning for International Business Negotiation* (Cambridge, Mass.: Ballinger, 1974).

If the sale of the stock of foreign banks is spread over a decent period of time, I do not see any difficulty for the capital market to absorb this new flotation.

The micro-effects on the structure of the banking industry were also mentioned:

We are aware that one of the risks of this measure is possibly to generate a higher income concentration in the hands of the few financial groups which will be able to buy the stocks of foreign banks. There are other alternatives. Some new institutions have to be created.

On the external effects, such as the obtaining of international loans or the possibility of a substantial decrease in the flow of foreign investment, Colombian government officials seemed not especially worried:

The negative effect on foreign investment will be offset by the comparatively attractive assets of Colombia as a host country: political stability, economic growth, low-cost manpower, size of the market. Anyway, the government does not want foreign investment in all areas.

If some banks are leaving the country, others will be anxious to syndicate our international operations; we have at present twenty-six to thirty-five international banks willing to lend us money.

Nevertheless, we are aware that the international financial community will be tempted to put pressure on us and we are very careful in our dealing with its representatives.

Domestic bankers were concerned by the effects of the decree, in particular fearing measures of retaliation overseas and economic effects internally:

Colombian banks which wish to expand overseas are likely to receive an unfriendly treatment.

If one or more foreign banks leave or reduce their interests in Colombia, that will not be so good for Colombia, because a bank which has an investment here will be more willing to help in case of difficulties than another one, not as well informed.

We oppose the measure because we want to be welcomed overseas.

Colombia's treatment of banks will not influence the other Andean countries, except Ecuador.

Foreign bankers had a much more pessimistic view of the measure. The virtually unanimous opinion was that there would be negative effects for Colombia of one or more of the following kinds: the decree would further discourage private foreign investors; it would make less Colombian capital available for other domestic investments; and it would contribute to the credit squeeze and balance of payments problems. To illustrate:

Since banking is tied into the whole economy, many other economic issues are involved, such as the balance of payments, the inflation rate, etc. The banks are part of a larger picture.

The timing is not good for the general economic situation in Colombia, especially the shortage of credit.

Buying foreign bank stock would reduce the money available for investment in other needed domestic projects.

American investors are wary of Colombia now even though they are aware of its great potential.

Other foreign investors are watching what happens to the foreign banks.

Other investors won't be influenced by what's happening in the banking sector because it's special, like mining.

The decree will hurt the foreign investment picture.

I'm basically pessimistic at this time, but I've lived through several cycles.

Foreign investment is down sharply in the last several years due to the Andean Pact. The recent decree is in line with the Pact and will further discourage interest from investors.

The present foreign banks are top flight world banks and are an asset to Colombia due to their contacts and influence on foreign investors and investments.

On the long-range effects on the foreign banks themselves, there was concern over such ramifications as the perceived drawbacks of having a "mixed" status. Moreover, since Colombia is a widely respected and influential country in Latin America, what happens there was seen as having significant effects elsewhere, as well as in the possible future changes in Colombian requirements for other multinational firms (the "opening wedge" viewpoint).

We are not sure of the extent to which the economic consequences of this measure have been evaluated. To our knowledge, the existing studies on the topic are limited. (See the appendix for summaries of some analyses of likely effects of this decision.) Of course the economic consequences will vary according to the degree and means of implementation of the decree. One problem in implementation is whether there exists a desire on the part of national interests to buy the stocks of foreign banks.

Are Colombian investors interested in buying the stock of the foreign banks? The question of the conversion of foreign banks into "mixed" enterprises is complex. Government officials were aware of the issue—whether there exists a domestic capacity for absorbing this new capital in the Colombian stock market.

> We think that if the stocks of foreign banks are presented to the capital market within a fairly extended period, over ten years for instance, there will be no problem.

> The government is not interested in buying the stock of foreign banks.

The possibility of intervening to foster the conversion process was not excluded:

> If there is any problem on the demand side of the stock of foreign banks, we might grant fiscal incentives to national investors to allow the stock market to compete with UPACs.[74]

Some domestic bankers were also not especially worried by this issue; others were aware of the weakness of the stock market:

> With time, this capital increase will be absorbed easily. Foreign banks are good investments. Some financial groups which have no banking network are longing to control them.

> Our bank which is trying to increase its capital base is experiencing some difficulties in selling new stocks on the stock market especially because of the present depression of the stock market due, among other things, to the new taxes put on dividends. So we think it will also be difficult for foreign banks.

The foreign bankers had in the main a pessimistic view of the process. The vast majority of foreign bankers interviewed—both from banks with and without branches—believed either that there was not enough local capital available and interested or at least that there is no guarantee that it would be available. Both views led to a feeling of uncertainty:

> Groups have already approached us to invest in our bank, but there's no guarantee all banks could sell the required amount of their stock.

---

[74] UPAC is a bond which is indexed to inflation and gives an additional return of 5 percent within a maximum limit of 25 percent interest rate.

There isn't enough local capital that wants to buy into foreign banks.

Not sure enough local capital wants to buy into foreign banks.

Many Colombian banks are under-capitalized now, hence do not have funds to buy stock of foreign banks.

The government will buy in; there are no other funds available.

I see no problem in foreign banks selling their stock to Colombians. It's a good investment. Many are interested.

On the type of investor likely to buy, several preferences for non-banking investors were expressed so that the present banking expertise and direction could continue as the contributions of the foreign bank to the joint venture.

On the general issue, the views differed between government officials and foreign investors. The government expressed a belief that the capital market would absorb the new issues of bank stock; foreign investors were more worried. Moreover, a distinction has to be made between the representatives of foreign banks with no branches in Colombia who answered the question in theory only, and the representatives of the foreign banks which have branches in Colombia, who spoke from quite practical concerns.

The government is apparently aware that it will have to do something beyond what it has done, and it may be assumed that specific plans will be designed on an emergency basis if they are really needed. Otherwise, foreign banks and domestic investors will be left to their own negotiations. These negotiations will involve the thorny problem of stock valuation.

What are the problems of stock valuation? The problem of stock valuation lies near the center of the whole process of conversion of ownership and the definition of the role of the government. So far, the government has clearly defined its policy:

The institution competent to authorize the conversion process is the planning board.

We are aware of the complexity of the issue; it is not the role of the government to be involved in stock valuation. There are many factors to consider, and the best persons who can evaluate the variables are the parties involved themselves. Our role will be to see if the methodology used is coherent. In principle, we will not intervene in the stock valuation process itself.

Domestic banks take the point of view of the government.

> Government should not intervene in the negotiations of stock valuation; it is the role of private enterprise.

Foreign banks are concerned about stock valuation in the event of distorted supply in the stock market created by forced conversion to Colombian ownership:

> As we are legally required to convert ourselves, the supply of stocks will exceed the demand and the price of our stocks will inevitably fall.

> What we generally do are several valuations: value of the stock based on past profitability, on expected growth of earnings, on base value with an appreciation for good will, and we take a weighted average of these valuations.

> It takes time to evaluate stock, but we can arrive at an agreed figure.

> Every foreign banker has quite an accurate idea of what his bank is worth.

When we interviewed representatives of well-known international auditing firms, they indicated that they could certify a balance sheet, but that it is the company that must evaluate its good will and profit prospects:

> What could be possible in case of difficulties is that each of the two parties involved appoint an independent firm to assess their value and that these firms negotiate.

Is some additional mechanism needed to improve the dialogue between the government and foreign banks? Government officials must, of course, be aware that the foreign banking issue is "touchy." They see the risks of their being subjected to various pressures, but they suggested that further information given to the public could help to resolve the issue and that they would welcome serious objective studies on the topic. On the other hand, they were aware that, in a negotiating position, they should, in most instances, retain any confidential information which might contribute to polemic.

Although local bank respondents believed that the dialogue with government had normally been quite good, the foreign bank respondents were evenly split on this seventh question. One half said the Banking Association had provided an adequate channel of communication. The other half thought that some additional channel was needed to improve communication with the government. All, however, complimented the Banking Association and said that it in no way discriminated against foreign banks. For example:

The bankers' association is more active than in most other countries.

The Banking Association is a good channel for dealing with bank-government problems.

I have recommended before that foreign banks should have some other means of communication with the government.

The Superintendent of Banks is very open and easily reached.

The lines of communication are there. We're just not getting the information we need.

The banking decree came without any advance warning.

Communication between foreign banks and the government definitely needs improving.

What are the most likely negotiating procedures? The government has suggested that foreign banks would wish to negotiate jointly. Some government officials remarked:

We think we are not going to grant exceptions to the rules as Venezuela did with first class banks, but if a foreign bank can prove its contribution to the country, it will be a plus for it.

We are very careful to avoid any pressure from any one.

So far, the reaction of public opinion has been quite favorable to us.[75]

Domestic firms thought the issue was so complex that it would take time to resolve:

Our understanding is that the negotiation will take time and the delay will be important and necessary. It is also possible that the negotiation will be distinct for each bank, granting different delays to each of them.

If some banks leave the country, it will require at least three to five years.

The legal problem of converting a branch to a new corporation should take no more than six months.

Foreign firms generally appeared to think that they should negotiate separately:

Each bank has its own history, its own nationality, and is contributing differently to the country. It should therefore be treated separately.

[75] See, for instance, the articles published in *El Tiempo* by Carlos Caballero Argaez, "La Colombianización Financiera," May 23, 1975, p. 5A, and Jorge Valencia Jaramillo, "Los Bancos Extranjeros," June 17, 1975, p. 5A.

Our bank has contributed highly to the training of Colombian bank officers, to the morality and fair play of bank operations, to regional development, and to export promotion. We have to receive a negotiated treatment which satisfies the Colombian policy and our bank objectives.

If we are converted rapidly, we may lose important sums.

The more discreet the public opinion and the university professors on the issue, the better.

The views expressed here are interesting. Normally, one would expect that the government would prefer to negotiate with each bank separately and that the foreign community would prefer to negotiate as a united front. In this case the government was expecting a request for joint negotiation while the foreign banks preferred separate negotiations.

Can neutral observers play a useful role in this situation? [76] The responses on this point were likely biased in a positive direction from the courteousness of the respondents. We would probably be accurate in concluding that the attitude was one of "wait and see." However, when a written report was mentioned, there usually was immediate interest expressed in seeing it.

A substantive comment was made by one individual who has had banking experience in several countries:

A useful function of a third party study can be to call attention to how the problem at issue fits into the larger picture; it can help bring perspective to the situation.

With this in mind, it is time for us to summarize and to present our recommendations. In doing so, we do not intend to favor any particular viewpoint on these issues—not the point of view of the government, or of the domestic banks, or of the foreign banks.

4. A LOOK AHEAD AND SOME RECOMMENDATIONS

A foundation has been laid for a look ahead. We have reviewed many of the events out of which the immediate issues have arisen. We have sought the current views of individuals closely concerned with Decree 295 in "off-the-record" interviews. Their views and perceptions have been summarized and illustrated with quotations identified only by reference group. We may now take a brief look at each of the issues around which the interviews were conducted.

---

[76] Obviously, this question is best answered by an after-the-fact assessment of what effects occurred that could be related to this kind of third party endeavor.

Looking Ahead. The importance of Decree 295 can best be determined by considering the possible interactive effects of the decree within the country's economy, along with the "ripple" effects the decree may have both within and outside Colombia. If this decree were followed by others affecting other business sectors, and if other Latin American countries were influenced by what Colombia has done, then obviously the decree would have an importance beyond its importance for the six banks directly involved. And even for these banks it could certainly have an effect on their branches in other countries.

The reasons the government initiated a change in the status of foreign banks when it did can be summed up (in an overly simplified manner) by saying it was a political decision. But when what is meant by the word "political" is explored, the reasons become many and complex.

For example, one important influence is the Andean Pact.[77] What happens within the framework of the pact in the future will, in turn, affect what Colombia does in relation to multinationals in particular and to foreign investments in general. A second influence is the widespread negative attitude toward an excess of non-Colombian influences—an attitude symbolized by the word "dependencia."[78]

Interest in the government's long-range goals is as understandable as those goals are difficult for democratically elected governments to define except in the short term. However, the fact that the goals relevant to multinationals, and more particularly to the foreign banks, do not seem at all clear to many of those involved with the banks creates a heightened sense of uncertainty, and the presence of uncertainty normally causes investors to require a high potential rate of return for participation in any venture.

Among the many possible internal effects of the decree are those on the supply of local capital, the stock market, the balance of payments, the degree of concentration of banking interests, the attitude of foreign banks toward Colombia, and the influence of these banks on other foreign investors. Because many of these are either short-term effects or relatively minor, with time and proper handling they can no doubt be accommodated.

---

[77] Carlos Caballero Argaez and François Lombard, "Origen, Presente y Futuro de la Decision 24 del Grupo Andino," presented at the seminar on Transnational Enterprise, Hotel Hilton, July 31, 1975, Bogotá, Colombia.

[78] See, for example, Sunkel, "Big Business and Dependencia," *Foreign Affairs*, vol. 50, no. 3 (April 1972). An empirical test of dependency theory is described in John Walton, "Economic Development and Dependency Theory: Some Observations from a Comparative Study of Urban Regions," in *Latin American-U.S. Economic Interactions*, eds. Robert B. Williamson, et al. (Washington, D. C.: American Enterprise Institute for Public Policy Research, 1974), pp. 367-375.

However, second only to what the government does officially by decrees and laws is the manner or way in which it implements them; the "music" is heard and felt as keenly as the "tune." For example, the manner in which representatives of the government handle their contacts and relationships with representatives of the foreign banks will have an effect on the banks' attitudes and decisions, both now and in the future. Traditional Colombian courtesy and diplomacy could be a definite asset here.

The problems raised by the valuation of foreign bank stock and the extent of interest Colombians may have in purchasing the stock add to the climate of uncertainty, especially for the banks directly involved. These are not insurmountable problems, but they do exist.

Communication between the government and the foreign banks, regardless of its past level, could always be improved. Generally speaking, communication can only be ensured if it is planned for: hence the possibility of improving future communication by trying out some additional mechanism, channel, or forum seems well worth consideration. Moreover, an open discussion and sharing of viewpoints and ideas is a realistic road toward improving both the understanding and the quality of the decisions of all parties involved.[79] While openness is no panacea and while it is not risk-free, it is nevertheless the soundest operating policy in the long run. If some participants feel that by open and informal discussion they might be exposing themselves to added pressures, that is one of the risks.[80] On the other hand, formal negotiation (though a specific and limited type) is an important type of communication, and it must certainly take place fairly shortly in the wake of Decree 295.

The Multiple Goal Model. Let us now broaden this discussion by placing these immediate issues in their larger setting. By employing contemporary administrative concepts, we may increase our understanding of some key factors in a complex and possibly confusing reality. All available wisdom must be used if people and their organizations are to shape or influence the future as well as adjust to it.

All organized activities are goal directed, be they the activities of a professional group, a business, or a government. Whether the

[79] This is a scientific principle supported by ample research and extensive practical experience. See, for example, Norman R. F. Maier, *Problem Solving Discussions and Conferences* (New York: McGraw-Hill, 1963).

[80] For a discussion of the evolving stages of dialogue between host governments and multinational firms, see Howard V. Perlmutter, "The Perplexing Routes of Legitimacy: Codes of Conduct for MNE's Regarding Technology Transfer and Development," *Stanford Law Review* (in press).

goals are clear and explicit or not, they exercise a profound influence over the plans and strategies that are carried out in the real world to achieve those ends. Usually, organized activities have multiple goals. This introduces a major complication because it would be as unlikely as a solar eclipse that several goals would be completely compatible with each other and point in precisely the same direction, and in fact multiple goals are generally more or less in conflict with one another. That is to say, achieving one optimally reduces the achievement of another; the resources committed to one make less available for another, and so on.

The Colombian government appears to have at least three major long-range objectives. Assuming all three are of top priority, the order of listing is not important. One goal is to control inflation as effectively as possible. A second is to develop the economy and improve the general welfare of the people as rapidly as possible. The third is to be as self-reliant and independent as possible, "to stand on one's own feet," and to have maximum control of those decisions that affect the country's future. These goals are clear, understandable, and generally shared by all the nations of the world.

The sobering reality is that these goals interfere with one another and that it is not possible to maximize all three at the same time, however much one might wish to do so. Some of the implications of this conceptual model of reality are fairly certain and they are relevant to Colombia as well as to other countries.

If the second and third goals were pulling in exactly opposite directions, it would be a "win-lose" situation and a country would have to settle for one or the other; fortunately, this is not the case. If these two goals were so nearly in line that the interaction effects were insignificant, attention could shift to other matters. But if they are somewhere between these two extremes, which surely they are, then to use the popular expression, the policy makers "have to earn their pay." They are forced to consider such difficult and subjective questions as these: How much effect do our efforts to achieve one have on the other (in other words, what are the trade-offs involved)? What is the optimum that can or is likely to be achieved by both? Or, alternatively, what is acceptable for one so the other can be maximized?

How does all this apply to the question of Decree 295? The decree is aimed at helping achieve the self-reliance or independence goal,[81] but it will have some effects on the economic development

---

[81] That is why the decree is widely considered a "political" rather than an "economic" decision.

and welfare of the country in both the short and long run. It may be asked: how much progress toward self-reliance and self-respect is minimally sufficient (for general mental health and political stability) so that the pressing public needs for economic health and the other development objectives of the country can be maximized? How this question is answered is for the policy makers and political leaders to decide. The role of the research scholar is to clarify the issues and increase the options available to those who make and interpret public policy.

Multinational firms also have multiple goals to be achieved at acceptable levels, goals which vary from firm to firm.[82] For the multinational banks to reach an agreement with the Colombian government, there must be a mutual or common interest, and each party needs to be aware of the minimal requirements of the other. A fairly safe, if politically controversial, prediction is that in Third World countries, majority ownership by a foreign firm, especially in the vital banking sector, will not meet one of the minimum requirements of the government and the public. Hence, sooner or later the firms involved will have to sell at least 51 percent of their stock to local stockholders. Colombia appears to have reached this position officially in the banking sector in 1975, and the position is not likely to change.

The questions then become when, how, and under what circumstances? If our analysis is reasonably accurate, the foreign banking firms should avoid engaging in any wishful thinking and should try to work out a mutually acceptable agreement with the government. An alternative would be for the Colombian Congress to pass a law which could be more restrictive and unfavorable to the foreign banks than Decree 295.

For private firms, the basic decision criterion is: What is best for the several constituencies that must be satisfied—the stockholder owners, the business clients who receive the services, the employees including managers, the resident community and country? (This criterion applies to domestic and multinational firms alike.) For a government, the basic decision criterion is: What is best for the people in the short and the long run? On these two criteria must be based the resolution of the problems involved in Colombia's treatment of foreign banks.

---

[82] The view used for convenience by some economists that the only goal worth considering for a private firm is its "profit" has been merely a simplified way of viewing reality in order to deal quantitatively with firms in various economic theories and principles. However, to the extent the public has been thus "educated" to think that profit is in fact the only goal of a business, a significant public disservice has been rendered, albeit unintentionally.

Points Based on Analyses Summarized in the Appendix. First, the government should be aware of the indirect effects of the foreign banks. There can be ways of increasing these indirect contributions (transfer of administrative skills or creation of new types of services) without the increase being subject to the whole "package" of factors involved in a foreign investment—factors such as technology, capital, and management control. Second, the government must be aware that the effect on the stock market would be quite negative if a required public offering of stock for Colombian ownership were to be carried out in one year. A longer period (such as ten years) for the Colombianization of foreign banks would greatly reduce this negative impact. Third, the government should, in principle, not intervene in the evaluation of the stock of foreign banks. It should intervene if the evaluation seems out of line with the book value, or the registered dollar amount of stock, because there might be some ways of repatriating unearned capital that could place a strain on the balance of payments. Finally, the government should be aware that while in theory the legal conversion of foreign banks does not offer special difficulties, nevertheless, if all foreign banks were to convert at the same time, there would be administrative problems at the Banking Superintendency, and special instructions should be given to ease this potential problem.

Recommendations. For the appropriate discussions to be carried out, it would appear that foreign bankers expect and need from government officials a series of assurances:

First, they should receive more definitive statements than they have on the future policy of the government toward foreign investment and foreign banks. The views expressed here can serve as background information. The impact of such statements would be to help the home offices of individual firms to finalize their decisions, and to demonstrate that there are clear rules for the treatment of foreign investment in Colombia. Colombian policy is obvious in the minds of some government officials, but foreign investors seem to be misinterpreting it. Second, the government should express its views on the related questions raised: What will be the effect on balance of payments, and on the capital market? What happens if foreign banks do not find any buyers? What should be the timing of the conversion process? Third, the foreign banks need assurance that there will not be a major cost if the government negotiates with each bank separately rather than jointly.

Foreign investors, on the other hand, should demonstrate their contribution to Colombia on such bases as the transfer of administrative skills, job creation, export promotion, regional development, the use of financial resources, and contribution to national income and balance of payments. The more technical and comprehensive the negotiations, the lower will be the risk of misunderstanding, or informal pressure, and the more beneficial the effect for the welfare of the country as a whole.

APPENDIX: SUMMARIES OF SUPPLEMENTARY ANALYSES

This appendix consists of three summaries of more extensive analyses. The recommendations based on this supplementary information are on page 54.

Economic Evaluation of the Costs and Benefits of the Colombianization of Foreign Banks.
We have used a small econometric model, first prepared by H. C. Bos and J. Tinbergen.[83] The possible effects of the Colombianization of foreign banks are numerous:

Effect on balance of payments. If the dividend repatriation be curbed in the future by 50 percent or 100 percent in case of departure of the foreign banks, thus improving the balance of payments, other effects are likely to appear—effects such as a decrease in capital inflow of new foreign investment, decrease in the action of export promotion done by these banks, and repatriation of capital of the latter.

Effect on national income. Using United Nations Industrial Development Organization methodology, we come up with a result indicating a minor direct role of foreign banks as far as value-added generation in the form of salaries, taxes, and earnings amounting to 0.14 percent of the Colombian GNP. Therefore, the foreign banks have a minor direct effect on Colombia's growth. However, the qualitative impact or contribution should be analyzed in detail.

Effect on job creation. This effect is hard to evaluate. Our evaluation is that foreign banks are employing directly 2,200 persons. Evaluating the indirect effect is difficult, and each bank should help.

Effect on income distribution. It is hard to evaluate the effect on income distribution using Gini or Lorenz curves. The ratio of

---

[83] H. C. Bos and others, *Private Foreign Investment in Developing Countries,* International Studies in Economics and Econometrics (Dordrecht, the Netherlands: D. Reidel Publishing, 1974).

wages to profits is equal to 56 percent, which shows that the share of employees is important and that these banks are contributing to income distribution. Another variable is the use of the taxes paid as a tool for income distribution. A final possible factor would be to analyze bank lending policy, whether the resources are going to a limited number of privileged firms or to a broader public. This is in itself a whole study that we cannot do here.

To conclude, quantitatively the role of foreign banks is apparently discrete and minor; 0.14 percent of GNP is a severely limited figure. Qualitatively, foreign banks can transfer technology, bring a new philosophy of international banking, and be the window of Colombia internationally, but it is up to each bank to prove its contribution.

The Colombianization of Foreign Banks and the Colombian Capital Market. The Colombian stock market is small (6 percent to 8 percent of transferable savings) and currently weak. Its size is $64.5 million (U.S.). If one considers that a conservative estimate of the assets of foreign banks is $22.5 million (U.S.), one can measure the problem of absorption of foreign bank shares by the Colombian capital market.

This image is not quite adequate. Foreign banks will presumably sell only 51 percent of this amount, that is, $11.5 million (U.S.). Also the sale need not be in a year but could be over a ten-year period, and the capital market would have to absorb $1.15 million (U.S.) annually. Foreign banks are likely to offer part of their stocks privately and part publicly. If they offered 60 percent of their new stocks publicly, the annual flotation would be $.65 million (U.S.), which is a reasonable amount to be issued without problems in the stock market.

The problem of stock valuation has been briefly mentioned. The degree of difficulty in valuation depends on the strategy of the banks and the delay they are given in liquidating their assets.

Legal and Fiscal Issues Involved. The legal conversion of foreign banks is a process quite well known. The Banque Nationale de Paris did it in 1972. It took three to five months, without including the financial negotiations between the two partners.

Cover and book design: Pat Taylor